Smithsonian

LITTLE EXPLORER

# SPACE

by Martha E. H. Rustad

CAPSTONE PRESS
a capstone imprint

Little Explorer is published by Capstone Press,
1710 Roe Crest Drive, North Mankato, Minnesota 56003
www.capstonepub.com

**For Leif and Markus, for always telling me to look at
the sky. —MEHR**

**Library of Congress Cataloging-in-Publication Data**
Rustad, Martha E. H. (Martha Elizabeth Hillman), 1975-
 Space / by Martha E.H. Rustad.
   p. cm. — (Smithsonian little explorer)
 Audience: K-3.
 Summary: "Introduces space to young readers,
including our solar system, other stars, the universe, and
space travel"—Provided by publisher.
 Includes index.
 ISBN 978-1-4765-0251-9 (hardcover)
 ISBN 978-1-4765-3545-6 (paper over board)
 ISBN 978-1-4765-3551-7 (paperback)
 ISBN 978-1-4765-3557-9 (ebook PDF)
 1. Astronomy—Juvenile literature. 2. Solar system—
Juvenile literature. I. Title.
 QB46R87 2014
 520—dc23                    2012050591

**Editorial Credits**
Kristen Mohn, editor; Sarah Bennett, designer; Eric Gohl,
media researcher; Kathy McColley, production specialist

Our very special thanks to Andrew K. Johnston,
Geographer, Center for Earth and Planetary Studies,
National Air and Space Museum, Smithsonian
Institution, for his curatorial review. Capstone would
also like to thank Kealy Wilson, Smithsonian Institution
Project Coordinator and Product Development Manager,
and the following at Smithsonian Enterprises: Ellen
Nanney, Licensing Manager; Brigid Ferraro, Director
of Licensing; Carol LeBlanc, Senior Vice President,
Consumer & Education Products.

**Image Credits**
Capstone: 17 (top); iStockphotos: Chris Crafter, 5 (top);
NASA: 16 (front), 26, 27 (top), 28, 29, ESA/M. Livio and
the Hubble Heritage Team, 13 (bottom), JPL, 19 (top
right), JPL/Cornell, 19 (bottom right), 27 (bottom), JPL/
Northwestern University, 18 (bottom); Newscom: WHA/
United Archives/KPA, 5 (bottom); Science Source: BSIP,
12–13, Victor Habbick Visions, 14–15; Shutterstock:
Anatolii Vasilev, 22–23 (back), Antony McAulay, 18
(top), 19 (top left, middle right, bottom left), 20 (all), 21
(all), Cardens Design, 1, 7 (back), Denis Tabler, cover,
Dr_Flash, 22 (bottom), fotosutra.com, 32, godrick, 6,
Gunnar Assmy, 22 (top), Igor Kovalchuk, 18–19 (back),
20–21 (back), Johan W. Elzenga, 25 (bottom), lolya1988,
25 (back), Luka Veselinovic, 7 (front), 10 (front), Morgan
Lane Photography, 17 (bottom), My Good Images, 16–17
(back), Ola-ola, 9 (front), peresanz, 4–5 (back), SNEHIT,
19 (middle left), Stephen Girimont, 30–31, Tjeffersion,
8¬–9, Vibrant Image Studio, 10 (back), xfox01, 11,
Yuriy Kulik, 4 (front); Wikipedia: ESO/L. Calçada/
Nick Risinger (skysurvey.org), 23 (bottom), Philipp
Salzgeber, 24

Design Elements: Shutterstock

Printed in the United States of America in Brainerd, Minnesota.
032013      007721BANGF13

# TABLE OF CONTENTS

# THE SKY

Look at the sky.
What do you see?
At night we see the
moon and stars.

During the day
we see the sun.

# WHAT ELSE IS OUT THERE IN SPACE?

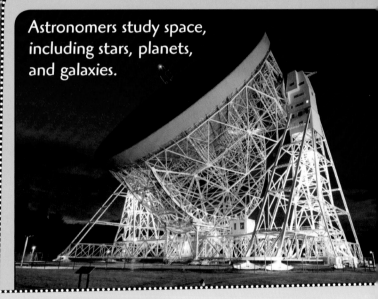

Astronomers study space, including stars, planets, and galaxies.

In 1610 a scientist named Galileo looked through a new invention called a telescope. He saw moons around Jupiter. Today people still use telescopes to see the night sky more closely.

5

# THE MOON

The moon is about 238,900 miles (384,500 kilometers) away from Earth.

A moon is a large rock that orbits a planet.

Our moon goes around Earth about once each month.

The moon has been circling our planet for about 4 billion years.

6

# WHAT SHAPE IS THE MOON TONIGHT?

Each night the moon looks a little different. Each week we see a new phase of the moon.

MOON PHASES

full moon

new moon

The moon pulls on our planet. This pull moves ocean tides back and forth every day.

# STARS

Stars look like tiny lights in the night sky.

But stars are very big—much bigger than Earth. They look small because they are so far away.

Stars are gigantic balls of burning gases.

Constellations are like dot-to-dot pictures in the night sky.

People think these groups of stars look like animals or people.

# THE SUN

The sun is the closest star to Earth.

Heat from the burning sun warms our planet. Plants, animals, and people need sunlight to live.

Earth spins once each day.

The side facing the sun has day. The side facing away from the sun has night.

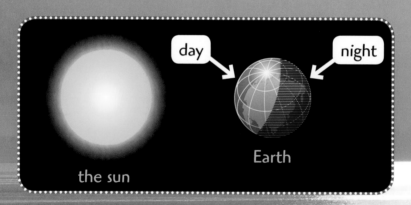

day

night

the sun

Earth

About **109 EARTHS** placed on top of each other would equal the height of the sun.

It takes about eight minutes for light from the sun to reach Earth.

# THE SOLAR SYSTEM AND MILKY WAY

The sun is the center of our solar system. Earth and seven other planets go around the sun.

The sun is just one star in the Milky Way galaxy. Hundreds of billions of stars shine in our galaxy.

"A GALAXY IS COMPOSED OF GAS AND DUST AND STARS—
BILLIONS UPON BILLIONS OF STARS."

—Carl Sagan, astronomer and writer

The universe holds
billions of galaxies.

Each one has millions or even billions of stars.

# THE UNIVERSE

There was a giant explosion almost 14 billion years ago.

Scientists call this the BIG BANG.

It was the beginning of our universe. Galaxies, stars, and planets later formed.

The universe is still
expanding, spreading
out the space
between galaxies.

# EARTH

Home, sweet home!
We live on the planet Earth.

Earth goes around the
sun once each year.
The path of this trip
is called an orbit.

Earth is tilted at an angle. For six months the northern half of Earth is tipped toward the sun. Summer happens on that part of the planet. The southern half is tipped away from the sun. It has winter. As Earth moves through its orbit, the seasons change.

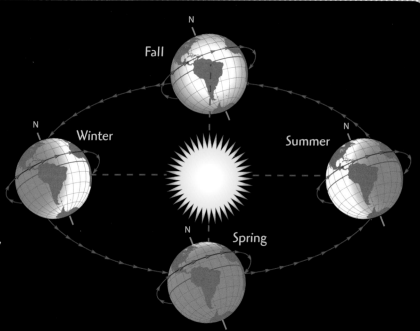

Fall

Winter

Summer

Spring

N

N

N

N

Gravity holds us to Earth. When you jump up, gravity pulls you back down. Without gravity, we would fly off into space.

# INNER PLANETS

The four planets closest to the sun are called the inner planets.

They have rocky surfaces.

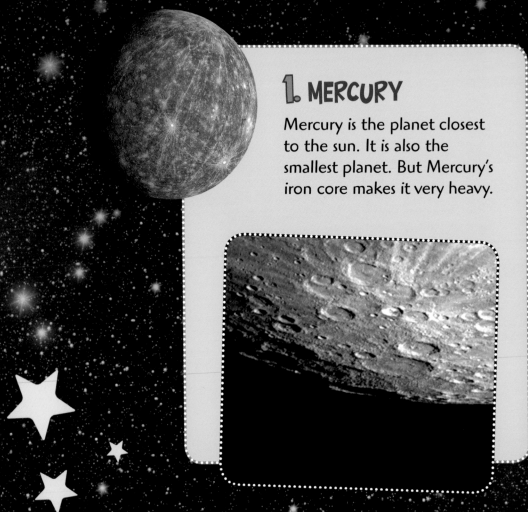

## 1. MERCURY

Mercury is the planet closest to the sun. It is also the smallest planet. But Mercury's iron core makes it very heavy.

## 2. VENUS

Temperatures on Venus reach 867 degrees Fahrenheit (464 degrees Celsius). Venus looks like a star in our night sky.

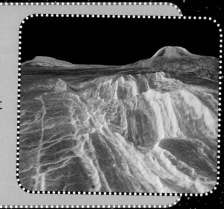

## 3. EARTH

Earth is the third planet from the sun. It's not too close to or too far from the sun. Earth is just right for people, animals, and plants to live.

## 4. MARS

From Earth, Mars looks like a red star. A year on Mars is twice as long as an Earth year.

# OUTER PLANETS

The four planets farthest from the sun are called the outer planets.

These gigantic planets are made mostly of gas.

## 5. JUPITER

Jupiter is the biggest planet. All the other planets could fit inside it! About 60 moons orbit Jupiter.

## 6. SATURN

Saturn has rings made of ice and dust. Titan is its largest moon.

## 7. URANUS

Uranus is tilted almost on its side. It has 13 faint rings and 27 moons.

## 8. NEPTUNE

Neptune's orbit is farthest from the sun. One trip around the sun lasts almost 165 Earth years.

## HOW LONG IS A YEAR?

A year is one trip around the sun. The length of a year is different on each planet.

| PLANET | NUMBER OF EARTH DAYS |
|---------|----------------------|
| Mercury | about 88 |
| Venus | about 225 |
| Earth | about 365 |
| Mars | about 687 |
| Jupiter | about 4,333 |
| Saturn | about 10,756 |
| Uranus | about 30,687 |
| Neptune | about 60,190 |

# SMALL WORLDS

Many thousands of smaller bodies orbit our sun. They weigh less than a planet.

Asteroids are smaller than planets. They are large pieces of rock and metal. An asteroid belt fills an area between the orbits of Mars and Jupiter.

Scientists think an asteroid hit Earth 65 million years ago. The crash would have made a lot of dust and clouds. The clouds may have blocked sunlight for years. Plants would have died. Dinosaurs died out soon after.

Small frozen worlds orbit our sun beyond Neptune. They are covered in ice and dust. Astronomers have discovered more than 1,000 so far.

Astronomers have named five objects dwarf planets: Ceres, Pluto, Haumea, Makemake, and Eris. They are smaller than planets but larger than most other tiny worlds in the solar system.

illustration of dwarf planet Makemake

# COMETS AND METEORS

Comets are chunks of rock and ice that orbit the sun.

They look like moving stars that grow tails when they near the sun.

Comets take years or even thousands of years to orbit the sun.

Comet Hale-Bopp shoots through the sky in 1997.

## EVER WISHED ON A SHOOTING STAR?

You were wishing
on a meteor.

A meteor is a space rock that
has gotten close to Earth.
The gases around our planet
burn meteors up.

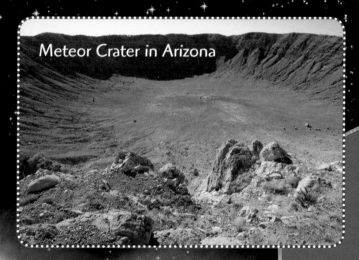

Meteor Crater in Arizona

Meteorites are
meteors from space
that land on Earth.

# SATELLITES, PROBES, AND ROVERS

A fast-moving light in the night sky might be a satellite.

Scientists launch satellites into orbit around Earth. Satellites gather information from space and send it back to us.

Scientists launch probes deep into space. Probes send back information about faraway planets and objects.

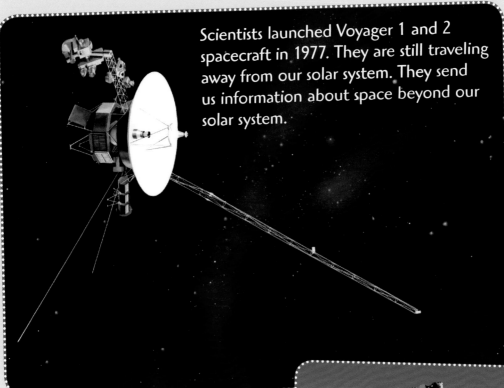

Scientists launched Voyager 1 and 2 spacecraft in 1977. They are still traveling away from our solar system. They send us information about space beyond our solar system.

Rovers are space robots that roam over other planets. They gather rocks and other items. They send signals back to scientists on Earth.

a Mars rover

# SPACE TRAVEL

Astronauts fly into space on spacecraft.
They study space and fix satellites.

Some astronauts live on the International Space Station. Astronauts train for years to learn how to travel in space.

WOULD YOU LIKE TO TRAVEL INTO SPACE SOMEDAY?

"THAT'S ONE SMALL STEP FOR A MAN, ONE GIANT LEAP FOR MANKIND."
—Neil Armstrong, the first human to walk on the moon

# GLOSSARY

**galaxy**—a large group of stars and planets

**gravity**—a force that pulls objects together; gravity pulls objects down toward the center of Earth; the sun's gravity pulls on Earth

**moon**—an object that orbits around a planet

**orbit**—to repeatedly move completely around another body; an orbit is also the path the object follows

**phase**—a stage; the moon's phases are the shapes that it appears to take over a month

**planet**—a large object that orbits a star

**rover**—a small vehicle that people can move by using remote control

**spacecraft**—a vehicle that travels in space

**star**—a ball of hot, bright, burning gases in space

**sun**—the star at the center of our solar system; the sun gives Earth light and warmth

**telescope**—a tool people use to look at objects in space; telescopes make objects look closer than they really are

# CRITICAL THINKING USING THE COMMON CORE

Stars are very big. Why do they look small to us? (Key Ideas and Details)

Look at the picture of the sun on page 11. How does the art compare the size of the sun to the size of Earth? (Craft and Structure)

Read Neil Armstrong's quote on page 29. Think about what Armstrong meant by "mankind." Then put the quote in your own words. (Integration of Knowledge and Ideas)

## READ MORE

**Bowman, Donna H.** *What Is the Moon Made Of?: And Other Questions Kids Have About Space.* Kid's Questions. Minneapolis: Picture Window Books, 2010.

**Conrad, David.** *Exploring Space.* Earth and Space Science. Mankato, Minn.: Capstone Press, 2012.

**Kortenkamp, Steve.** *Show Me Space: My First Picture Encyclopedia.* My First Picture Encyclopedias. Mankato, Minn.: Capstone Press, 2013.

## INTERNET SITES

FactHound offers a safe, fun way to find Internet sites related to this book. All of the sites on FactHound have been researched by our staff.

Here's all you do:

Visit *www.facthound.com*

Type in this code: 9781476502519

Super-cool stuff! Check out projects, games and lots more at
**www.capstonekids.com**

# INDEX